W9-CQD-305

Questions and Answers About

THE UNDERGROUND RAILROAD

HEATHER MOORE NIVER

PowerKiDS press.

NEW YORK

Published in 2019 by The Rosen Publishing Group, Inc.
29 East 21st Street, New York, NY 10010

First Edition

Editor: Heather Moore Niver
Book Design: Michael Flynn

Photo Credits: Cover SuperStock/Getty Images; cover, pp. 1, 3–20, 22–26, 28–32 (background) NuConcept Dezine/Shutterstock.com; pp. 5, 18 © AP Images; p. 7 Library of Congress Rare Book and Special Collections Division; pp. 9, 25 MPI/Archive Photos/Getty Images; pp. 10, 28 Everett Historical/Shutterstock.com; pp. 11, 15, 21, 27 courtesy of the Library of Congress; p. 13 (Levi Coffin) courtesy of the New York Public Library; p. 13 (map) adapted from the National Park Service map of escape routes of the Underground Railroad, NPS cartographic staff at Harpers Ferry Center; p. 17 Jeff Greenberg/Universal Images Group/Getty Images; p. 19 by Lake Erie Coastal Ohio, Inc.; p. 23 courtesy of Levi Coffin House Association and WayNet.org; p. 24 Stock Montage/Archive Photos/Getty Images; p. 29 © Interfoto/Alamy.

Cataloging-in-Publication Data

Names: Niver, Heather Moore.
Title: Questions and answers about the underground railroad / Heather Moore Niver.
Description: New York : PowerKids Press, 2019. | Series: Eye on historical sources | Includes glossary and index.
Identifiers: LCCN ISBN 9781538341322 (pbk.) | ISBN 9781538341315 (library bound) | ISBN 9781538341339 (6 pack)
Subjects: LCSH: Underground Railroad–Juvenile literature. | Fugitive slaves–United States–History–19th century–Juvenile literature. | Antislavery movements–United States–History–19th century–Juvenile literature.
Classification: LCC E450.N56 2019 | DDC 973.7'115–dc23

Manufactured in the United States of America

CPSIA Compliance Information: Batch #CS18PK: For Further Information contact Rosen Publishing, New York, New York at 1-800-237-9932

CONTENTS

REMEMBER THE RAILROAD

The **American Civil War** helped bring an end to slavery in the United States. To make that happen, many people risked their lives to help slaves in the South reach the safety of the northern states and Canada. This was very dangerous. Those who helped fugitive slaves faced fines and imprisonment. Slaves who were caught trying to escape faced much worse upon return to their owners.

To escape, a secret **network** called the Underground Railroad was used. The Underground Railroad wasn't an actual railroad—it was a network of people and places. Those who worked on the "railroad" were known as "conductors." They took in fugitive slaves, hid them, then helped them connect to the next "station." From there, another conductor would help them, on and on, until they were safely in the North.

SOME BUILDINGS ALONG THE
UNDERGROUND RAILROAD HAD
HIDDEN ROOMS AND HALLWAYS.
RUNAWAY SLAVES HID HERE
UNTIL IT WAS SAFE TO MOVE
TO THE NEXT PLACE ON THEIR
JOURNEY NORTH.

Sources from the Past

Throughout the United States, some houses and buildings from the 1800s have secret rooms and hiding places. Some even have tunnels beneath them. Conductors on the Underground Railroad would hide escaped slaves there. These places are artifacts, or things made by humans in the past that still exist today. We can learn a lot about the past

THE HORRORS OF SLAVERY

Even though the United States was founded on the ideas of liberty and equality, slave labor was still used there for centuries. Slave traders kidnapped Africans from their villages, forced them onto crowded ships, and brought them to America. They were then sold as slaves to landowners and merchants. Buying and selling human beings wasn't against the law. Some slaves were often treated no better than animals and were whipped, beaten, and even killed for small crimes.

Millions of black Americans worked as slaves on farms in the southern United States. They raised many crops, but one of the most important was cotton. Many proslavery groups believed the South's power and wealth depended on the free labor slaves provided. Not everyone thought this was a good idea.

Illustrations of the *American Anti-Slavery Almanac* for 1840.

"Our Peculiar Domestic Institutions."

Northern Hospitality—New-York nine months law. [The Slave steps out of the Slave State, and his chains fall. A Free State, with another chain, stands ready to re-enslave him.]

Burning of McIntosh at St. Louis, in April, 1836.

Showing how slavery improves the condition of the female sex.

The Negro Pew, or "Free" Seats for black Christians. | *Mayor of New-York refusing a Carman's license to a colored Man.*

Servility of the Northern States in arresting and returning fugitive Slaves.

Selling a Mother from her Child.

Hunting Slaves with dogs and guns. A Slave drowned by the dogs.

"Poor things, 'they can't take care of themselves.'"

Mothers with young Children at work in the field.

A Woman chained to a Girl, and a Man in irons at work in the field.

Branding Slaves.

Cutting up a Slave in Kentucky.

Paid. | *Unpaid.*

7

ABOLITION: ABSOLUTELY NO SLAVES

Before the Civil War, freeing a slave was against the law. Many Northerners, but also some people in the South, opposed slavery. They thought that no human being should own another. An antislavery movement began to grow. Antislavery **activists** were called abolitionists. "Abolition" means to end or destroy. Abolitionists wanted to outlaw slavery everywhere in the United States.

Some abolitionists started their own societies to help spread their message and further their cause. Many of these societies started their own newspapers. They were all about abolition. Other abolitionists, however, decided to take matters into their own hands. Some traveled to the South to help free slaves from their masters. They needed a way to safely and secretly transport, or move, escaped slaves to the North.

Read and Ponder

THE

FUGITIVE SLAVE LAW!

Which disregards all the ordinary securities of PERSONAL LIBERTY, which tramples on the Constitution, by its denial of the sacred rights of Trial by Jury, *Habeas Corpus,* and Appeal, and then enacts, that the Cardinal Virtues of Christianity shall be considered, in the eye of the law, as CRIMES, punishable with the severest penalties,—*Fines and Imprisonment.*

Freemen of Massachusetts, REMEMBER, That Samuel A. Elliott of Boston, voted for this law, that Millard Fillmore, our whig President *approved* it and the Whig Journals of Massachusetts sustain them in this iniquity.

HOWELL COBB,
Speaker of the House of Representatives.
WILLIAM R. KING,
President of the Senate protempore.
Approved September 18, 1850.
MILLARD FILLMORE.

Printed and For Sale at the Spy Job Office, Worcester, Mass.

Sources from the Past

The headline of this poster calls readers to think about the true cost of slavery. This is an actual poster that was hung on display in Massachusetts in 1850, which makes it a primary source for the Underground Railroad. What can we learn from this poster about the thoughts of abolitionists at this time?

PICKING UP STEAM

Fugitive slaves were sometimes hidden in the homes of people who believed they should help their fellow human beings. **Rumors** spread that a certain person in a certain town would help. Hearing this, an abolitionist who lived a few towns away would send fugitives to that person's "station." Sometimes, a guide helped them travel between safe houses. Other times fugitives had to take care of themselves.

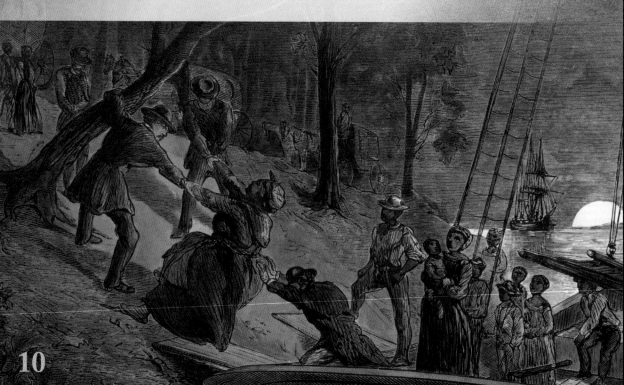

OVER TIME, A LOOSE NETWORK OF "SAFE HOUSES" WAS CREATED. THESE WERE THE HOMES OF ABOLITIONISTS WHO WANTED TO HELP FUGITIVE SLAVES ESCAPE TO FREEDOM. THE CROFT FARM, SHOWN HERE, IS A FORMER SAFE HOUSE ON THE UNDERGROUND RAILROAD IN CHERRY HILL, NEW JERSEY.

Abolition grew. More people became involved and began to communicate. Certain towns, many of which were near the Canadian border, became known as abolitionist hotspots. By the early nineteenth century, Canada had ruled that slaves who left their masters were free. Other groups began to form in New York, Philadelphia, and Boston. The tracks for the Underground Railroad had been laid.

CATCHING THE NEXT TRAIN

By the 1830s, trains were becoming a popular way to transport goods and people. Naturally, the Underground Railroad adopted the terms of this new, exciting form of American **transportation**. The people who helped slaves move between safe houses were known as conductors. Conductors helped slaves escape on foot, by boat, by horse and wagon, or even on actual trains. The homes and businesses where fugitives hid were called depots, or stations. The homeowners were known as stationmasters.

Important railroad **agents** were often given mock, or fake, titles. For example, Indiana resident Levi Coffin, who helped around 2,000 slaves reach freedom, was sometimes called the president of the Underground Railroad. As news of the growing railroad spread, slaves began to whisper about "catching the next train" north.

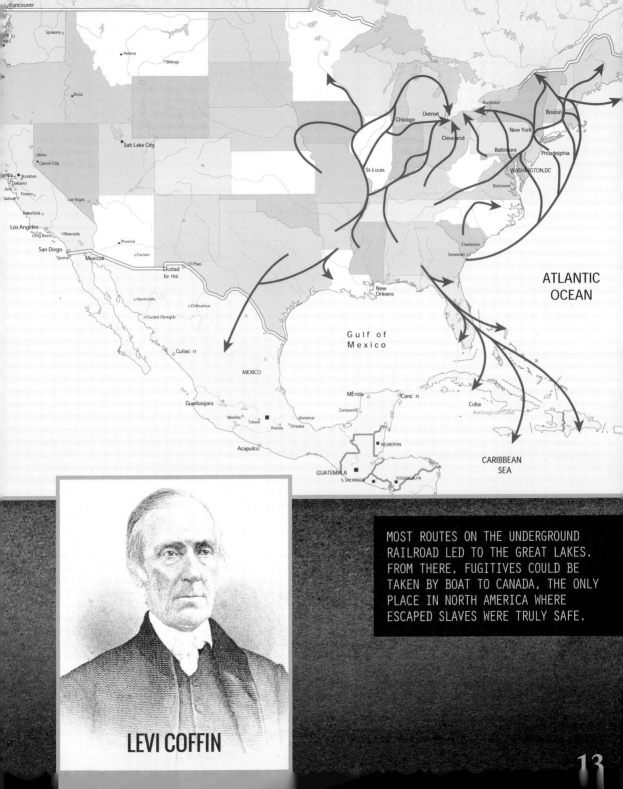

ATLANTIC
OCEAN

Gulf of
Mexico

CARIBBEAN
SEA

MOST ROUTES ON THE UNDERGROUND
RAILROAD LED TO THE GREAT LAKES.
FROM THERE, FUGITIVES COULD BE
TAKEN BY BOAT TO CANADA, THE ONLY
PLACE IN NORTH AMERICA WHERE
ESCAPED SLAVES WERE TRULY SAFE.

LEVI COFFIN

UNSAFE TRAVELS

Travel on the Underground Railroad was slow and dangerous. Stations were often no more than 20 miles (32 km) apart. This was considered the greatest distance runaway slaves could cover in one night, especially on foot. Sometimes, a group split up and stayed in separate shelters. This made it harder for slave hunters to track them. Agents of the railroad also found creative ways to mislead slave hunters.

Some slaves used clever tricks to escape to freedom. In 1849, Henry "Box" Brown was packed into a box addressed to the Philadelphia Anti-Slavery Society. All he had was a little bit of water, some crackers, and a tool with which he poked air holes into the box. Brown was shipped by wagon, boat, and railroad. He made it there alive.

HENRY "BOX" BROWN WAS A FUGITIVE SLAVE WHO MADE IT TO FREEDOM IN THE NORTH AFTER BEING SHIPPED IN A BOX FROM VIRGINIA TO PHILADELPHIA.

Sources from the Past

This illustration by Samuel Rowse was printed in 1850. Brown is shown coming out of his box, a free man in Philadelphia. James Kim and other abolitionists are shown looking surprised and happy that Brown survived the trip. The artist drew what they thought the moment may have looked like. Do you think this illustration is a primary source? Why or why not?

COSTUMES AND CODES

Secret codes were created so agents and slaves could communicate escape plans. For example, the word "shepherd" meant a conductor on the railroad was in the area. On the way north, news that "the wind blows from the south today" warned everyone that slave hunters were nearby.

Successful slave escapes depended on **disguises**. Blacks who had escaped earlier and returned to the South to help others escape often pretended to be slaves to draw less attention. A black man might dress himself in the clothes of a mourning widow. A black veil covered his face. A young black woman might cut her hair short, put on men's clothes, and pretend to be a laborer. These disguises helped them pass through society without anyone taking much notice.

MOST SLAVES HADN'T GONE TO SCHOOL AND FEW COULD READ, SO OTHER MEANS OF COMMUNICATION WERE NECESSARY. QUILTS WERE ONE OF THE MORE CLEVER METHODS USED TO GIVE FUGITIVE SLAVES INFORMATION ABOUT THE UNDERGROUND RAILROAD.

Sources from the Past

Quilts were hung in the open for slaves to see—like wash hanging on a clothesline to dry. Certain quilt patterns may have given information about the Underground Railroad. A quilted sailboat, for example, may have meant a boat was available in a nearby river. A monkey wrench pattern might mean it was time to collect the tools needed for an escape. Are these quilts primary sources? Why or why not?

MOTHER HUBBARD'S CUPBOARD

Agents along the Underground Railroad found ways to make their homes and businesses good hiding places for runaway slaves. Secret spaces were built where slaves could stay for days, weeks, and even months. Churches and abandoned buildings were sometimes turned into safe hiding places.

A SLAVE HIDEAWAY CAN STILL BE FOUND UNDER THE FLOOR AT THE LEWELLING QUAKER HOUSE UNDERGROUND RAILROAD MUSEUM IN SALEM, IOWA. THE HANDRAILS HAVE BEEN ADDED FOR SAFETY.

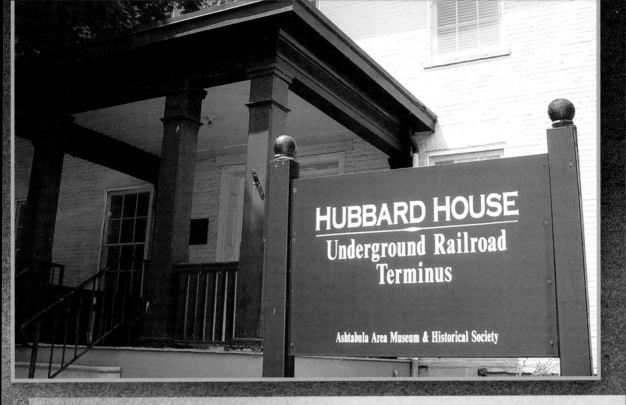

Tunnels and other escape routes were used to move fugitives quickly and secretly. Ohio abolitionist Colonel William Hubbard had a tunnel dug from his barn to the edge of nearby Lake Erie. Boat captains would wait there to carry slaves across the lake and into Canada. This station was sometimes referred to as Mother Hubbard's Cupboard. Edward Morris owned a two-story **tavern** in Pennsylvania that had seven staircases. If slave hunters showed up at the tavern, slaves could hide behind secret panels at the top of the staircases.

I CAN'T DIE BUT ONCE

Getting on the Underground Railroad was very dangerous. It was a journey toward freedom, but it meant taking incredible risks. Escaping slaves risked recapture and punishment. White conductors could be fined or put in jail for helping. Black agents in the North risked being caught and sold into slavery even though they were free. Those in the South risked their lives.

One African American conductor was Harriet Tubman. Tubman was an escaped slave who later joined the Underground Railroad. She may have helped rescue more than 300 runaway slaves, including members of her own family. By the mid-1850s, there was a $40,000 reward for her capture, a small fortune at the time. When asked why she risked her life again and again, Tubman would reply, "I can't die but once."

HARRIET TUBMAN REPEATEDLY RISKED HER FREEDOM BY RETURNING TO THE SOUTH. SHE MAY HAVE RETURNED AS MANY AS 19 TIMES TO LEAD ESCAPED SLAVES NORTH.

Sources from the Past

This picture of Harriet Tubman is believed to have been taken around 1880, years after the Civil War and the end of slavery. What can we learn about Tubman's life after slavery ended by studying this picture? Do you think this picture is a primary source?

PRESIDENT OF THE UNDERGROUND RAILROAD

Levi Coffin saw slaves for the first time in North Carolina when he was 7 years old. He never forgot the chained and handcuffed people. From that moment on he strongly opposed slavery.

In 1826, Coffin and his family moved to Newport, Indiana, and opened a general store. For the next 20 years, they helped more than 2,000 fugitives on their way to the next station on the railroad. Not one of the escaped slaves they aided was ever recaptured.

When the Coffins moved to Cincinnati, Ohio, they continued to help runaway slaves. Their large house could hide many fugitives. Some would hide upstairs for weeks. Other people who were staying in the house would have no idea they were there.

THE COFFIN FAMILY SOMETIMES HELPED SLAVES ALONG THE UNDERGROUND RAILROAD USING THEIR WAGON, WHICH HAD A SECRET HIDING SPACE BUILT IN.

TROUBLE BREWING

By the early nineteenth century, people on both sides of the slavery issue struggled to get what they wanted. The Missouri Compromise of 1820 was an attempt to please both sides. It said that a slave state couldn't be admitted to the Union without a free state also being admitted and vice versa. In addition, slavery wouldn't be permitted in any new U.S. territories north of Missouri's southern border.

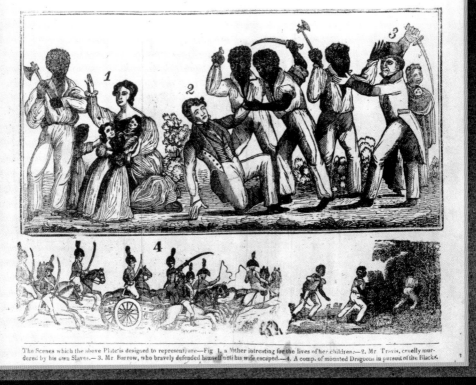

HORRID MASSACRE IN VIRGINIA.

The Scenes which the above Plate is designed to represent are—Fig 1, a Mother intreating for the lives of her children.— 2. Mr Travis, cruelly murdered by his own Slaves.— 3. Mr Barrow, who bravely defended himself until his wife escaped.— 4. A comp. of mounted Dragoons in pursuit of the Blacks.

TURNER WAS FOUND, TRIED FOR HIS CRIMES, AND HANGED. THE NAT TURNER **REBELLION** WAS THE WORST ACT AGAINST SLAVERY THE COUNTRY HAD EVER SEEN.

Meanwhile, trouble was brewing. Nat Turner, a religious slave from Virginia, told other slaves that he had visions of black and white angels fighting in heaven. In August 1831, Turner believed God wanted him to act. He and a group of 70 men stole guns and killed every white person they saw. They killed at least 55 people before they were stopped.

FRIGHT OF THE FUGITIVE SLAVE ACT

In 1850, Congress passed the Fugitive Slave Law. Fugitives could now simply be identified by the **affidavit** of a slave hunter and forcibly taken south without any further proof. Since they didn't need any proof that someone was a fugitive, slave hunters also couldn't be stopped from kidnapping free African American men and women.

The abolitionists were fired up. In December 1858, a slave went to abolitionist John Brown and asked him for help. He wanted his wife, children, and several other men to escape before they were sold by their master and separated forever. Brown organized an expedition that marched on two estates and liberated, or freed, the man and his family and the other slaves. From there, Brown and his men took the fugitives north to Canada.

OLD BROWN OF OSAWATOMIE,
AS JOHN BROWN WAS
SOMETIMES CALLED, BECAME A
NAME THAT AROUSED FEELINGS
OF TERROR AMONG THE
SUPPORTERS OF SLAVERY.

27

HORRORS AT HARPERS FERRY

On October 16, 1859, John Brown and a group of men attacked and captured a weapons-storage building in the town of Harpers Ferry, Virginia. The Virginia **militia** and U.S. Marines surrounded Brown and stormed the building on October 18. Ten of Brown's men were killed in the fighting, and seven—including Brown—were captured. Brown was found guilty of treason and hanged. His death made abolitionists want to rid the country of slavery by any means necessary.

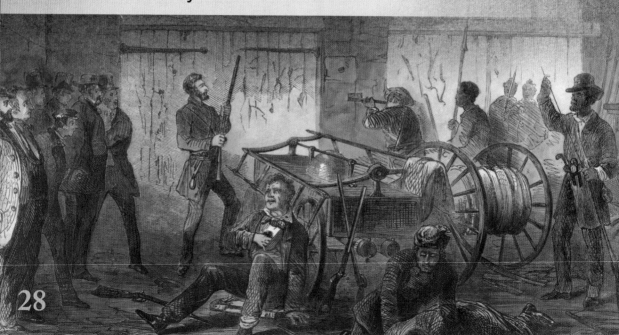

WHEN THE CIVIL WAR STARTED, MANY UNDERGROUND RAILROAD AGENTS WORKED TO HANDLE THE SUDDEN AND NOTICEABLE FLOOD OF SLAVES SEEKING FREEDOM. THIS IMAGE SHOWS A GROUP OF FUGITIVES BEING STOPPED AT THE BORDER BETWEEN THE SOUTH AND THE NORTH.

The 1850s marked the height of slaves escaping through the Underground Railroad. Then, on April 12, 1861, the Civil War began. Even more slaves began leaving the South, though they were still unsafe after reaching the North. Many Northern officers allowed slave hunters to take these fugitives back.

FINALLY, FREEDOM

The Underground Railroad was needed more than ever. When thousands of runaway slaves from the South headed north, the Underground Railroad finally went "above ground." Camps were set up, and **volunteers** helped feed and shelter the fugitives. Harriet Tubman helped, too. She even acted as a scout and spy for the Northern army.

In December 1865, Congress officially outlawed slavery by formally approving the Thirteenth Amendment to the U.S. Constitution. The Fourteenth Amendment, which followed in 1868, granted citizenship to all former slaves. The seemingly unreachable goal of freedom for all African Americans had finally been reached. The abolitionists' victory took a long time but the struggles and risks were worth it. With the help of the Underground Railroad, slavery had become a shameful part of America's past.

GLOSSARY

activist: Someone who acts strongly in support of or against an issue.

affidavit: A written report signed by a person who promises the information is true.

agent: A person who acts on behalf of another.

American Civil War: A war fought from 1861 to 1865 between the North and the South in the United States over slavery and other issues.

disguise: The clothes or other items that are worn so that people will not recognize you.

militia: A group of people who are not an official part of the armed forces of a country but are trained like soldiers.

network: People or groups that are closely connected and that work with each other.

rebellion: Open fighting against authority.

rumor: Information passed from person to person but has not been proven to be true.

tavern: A building that provides food and shelter for people who are traveling.

transportation: A way of traveling from one place to another.

volunteer: A person who does something to help because they want to do it.

INDEX

WEBSITES

Due to the changing nature of Internet links, PowerKids Press has developed an online list of websites related to the subject of this book. This site is updated regularly. Please use this link to access the list: www.powerkidslinks.com/eohs/railroad